Opposite the Tourbus

Sophia Walker

Burning Eye

This edition published by Burning Eye Books 2014

www.burningeye.co.uk
@burningeye

Burning Eye Books
15 West Hill, Portishead, BS20 6LG

ISBN 978 1 90913 642 7

For Adele, for putting up with me, and Kate, for turning my rants into poems. And to them both, for showing me what one of those home things is all about.

Advice 2:43

Smithy 2:52

Lessons in Intimacy 2:01

The Thin Blue Line 1:17

Dyke 1:49

Faggot 3:02

I'm Sorry You're Wrong 1:42

Relative Memory 2:01

Jump 1:39

Deserted Storm 1:47

Shades of Wrong or.... 0:57

Dear Douche Canoe 1:15

Values Meal 2:11

Two Faced Love 2:38

Lassie's Response 2:27

Asshole 2:18

On White People Saying Racism Is Dead in
America 1:49

Guilt 1:41

Moment of Silence 2:25

Afterwords 2:32

Lira 1:57

Seeds 1:18

House and Garden 2:16

When I was 21, a low paying internship meant I was broke and needed money for food. Obviously, as any normal person would, I wrote my first poem and entered a cash prize slam. I must be one of the only people to have entered poetry for the money. Definitely still broke. Oops. But along the way I've gotten to experience everything from performing in various parliaments to sharing a Greyhound bus seat across Utah with a drunk women who told me how she "accidentally" (air quotes hers, not mine) murdered someone with a coat hanger. Which is ideal conversation for 8:15 in the morning. Such are the adventures of life on tour. I've bathed in gas station sinks, survived on cheesy chips and instant coffee for inhumanly long, and slept on more sofas in more countries than my back cares to let me forget. At an open mic I very nearly didn't go to I even met my fiancee. Frankly, this poet life has been awesome (in the original sense). As I once texted my mum from the hard shoulder of a motorway next to a broken down Megabus on my first tour, "Look, mum! I'm a rockstar".

@poetwalker
www.facebook.com/SophiaWalker

Advice

When we were fifteen,
Ellie Famutimi scrawled
'If you're going through
hell, keep going'
on my bedroom wall.
For three years I stared
at that sentence every day.
I have read it on the insides
of my eyelids every time
I've shut my eyes ever since.
On the one occasion I risked
telling a therapist everything,
he said,
'I don't know how you've coped.
How do you keep going?'
At fifteen, Ellie Famutimi
was wiser than he.
I never tried therapy again.

Six years later, in a boggy,
tent-strewn, North Wales
mudpit at 4 am,
a heroin-addicted ex-convict
named Rich gifts me wisdom.
He says,
'Your parents are
just meant to provide
you with an example, so
I have to thank my father.
He showed me exactly
how not to be a dad.'
Rich is perceptive.
He's comprehended it's all
just perspective –

and perspective is
determined. How you
choose to view things is
deliberate.

The day I graduated high school,
the man I most look up to
gave me a card which said:
'Always travel in the direction
opposite to the tour bus.'
I have been stumbling through
scrubland ever since; this
relentless quest for the
adventurous has exposed me
to some harrowing things.
Aged twenty, I saw a village
massacred in front of me
in the middle of the night
and I –
I did nothing to stop it.

For nearly a decade
I felt guilty for my life.
There was no greater disrespect
I could've shown to the dead.
Self-indulgently I'd let myself
rewrite history 'til it was
all about me.
I didn't stop it.
I *couldn't* stop it.

I couldn't stop it.

How you choose to view
things is deliberate.
When going through hell,
keep going. You never
know when a slight perspective shift
reveals an unexpected side-exit.

Smithy

My highschool math teacher was Mr Smith
but we called him Smithy, all 5 foot 10,
weighing 140 dripping wet. He had smoker's teeth,
a visage too kind to be ugly, though definitely
not what our math class would call attractive.

One day in eleventh grade, Smithy chose to
teach us the Golden Ratio: 1 to 1.618,
the mathematical definition of beauty.
From a rectangle to Angelina Jolie,
though unconscious, it is the constant
similarity in everything we see as beautiful.

When we measured the distance
from forehead to nose, nose to chin,
Smithy's golden skin shaped him
the equation of gorgeous.

I have never once found true beauty where I expected.

When a too-long depression hit,
pushed me to its precipice,
I felt Smithy's vice grip pull
me back from that cliff before
I even knew he'd noticed.
I was not the only kid
he did this with.

1 to 1.618.
I trace the strain from all those
he saved in each of his
nicotine-stained teeth, his
grief for their misery.

He was mid-thirties but
his cheeks were lined with creases,
soft pleats in skin for each student
he couldn't mend. He never knew
how many of us he saved.

1 to 1.618.
At the school's wake Smithy's mother
sat in stunned silence, tears streaming
from her eyes but she was smiling.
There were over 500 alumni, some flying
thousands of miles; they stood up one by one
and told her how her son had shaped them.

1 to 1.618.

The sum total of seconds it took Smithy
to intervene if he could see someone in need.

The percentage of time he spent on him.

The probability any of us could do all he did.

One day in eleventh grade, Smithy chose to teach us
the Golden Ratio. It took me too long to see
he was the meaning of beautiful.

Lessons in Intimacy

It is a picturesque English village of
church coffee mornings, Women's Institute
baking glories; this is the kind of place
still happily engaging in Morris dancing.
Daily Mail dreamland, iconic cream-tea
land, this is where Enid Blyton's
Famous Five spend their vacation time.
This is idyllic England.

At 10 am, all lessons in session, the secondary
school is quiet. I find myself in a classroom
with twenty-seven youth; we are talking about sex.
Which in essence means we're speaking
'bout the internet. This discussion is governed
by the porn they've uncovered; 'lovers'
is a meaningless word in the world of
one cup and two girls. Hold firm…
There's an unmeant pun in those words,
not handjobs but the job at hand: stand
fast against the disheartening, this
desire to protect these pubescent kids
with no concept of what consensual is.

I ask them to define intimacy.
A girl of thirteen says 'anal sex'
and every classmember agrees.
'You see, you'd only have anal sex
with a boyfriend, but you'd give
a blowjob to anyone.'

This from kids too young to have
seen *Jackanory*. In a village of
church coffee mornings,
Women's Institute baking glories –
while grandmas make cream cakes
pre-teens brag how cream tastes,
trading glorious hot buttered rolls
for hot footage from glory holes.
                    This is
where innocence and the internet
intersect: the exact point
kids begin thinking
intimacy means anal sex.

The Thin Blue Line

Your heart stops for a second.
You age thirty years in two minutes
but you're still only nineteen
on the brink of a living nightmare
praying for the thin blue line.

It's the most undignified surroundings.
Stark, white tiles reflecting sharp, fluorescent light,
magnifying and illuminating the fear on your face
projected on a five-foot-wide rectangular mirror
praying for the thin blue line.

But the lack of dignity in all this taking place in a toilet
is hardly improved by the designer's requirements
that you then squat over and pee on a stick,
all the while praying for the thin blue line.

The sharp edges, hard floors and lack of company
that a toilet has a tendency to provide
prove somewhat of an obstacle
when you inevitably pass out upon
learning that despite all those prayers, negotiations
and desperate pleadings...

Perhaps because you were a Buddhist in middle school,
a Taoist in high school, and an atheist in college –

Perhaps because you got away with it one too many times and
    that's karma, baby –

Perhaps because it was exactly the wrong guy,
at exactly the wrong time, and that's tempting fate
just a little too much –

Perhaps there was a small hole in the condom,
and in your somewhat understandable haste
it just went unnoticed.

Perhaps for two hours as you lie on the
bathroom floor, unable to move, unable to breathe,
unable to do anything but stare at the ceiling and wonder
    'perhaps'.

But no amount of wondering will change the fact
that your prayers have gone unanswered and
what you see on that little, white, plastic stick
is not a thin blue line.

Dyke

To the man who repeatedly punched me,
stole all my money and spat 'dyke'
in my face with such vitriolic hatred
like it excused his behaviour,

Let's think about this for a second:
what is a dyke?

A sea wall.

A mere combination of stone and bonding agent
creating a haven against the forces of nature.

A few thousand metres
protect millions of people.
As if my arms could stretch with strength
in defence of all those who meant something
to me, could prevent them from drowning
when misfortune surrounds them,
a veritable life-raft in the face of
floods of days that shake us.

As if I were safety, never breaking
in the wake of waves of hatred.

I have stood the test of centuries
pushing back at me,
shaped strength against adversity,
made nations retract bigotry.
Please accuse me of holding back the sea.

With each punch he landed
his hate grew more candid
'til my mere act of standing
proved too much for his handling.

As he walked away with my money
and his bruised knuckles, I chuckled.

I'd learned I am more fearless than Perseus,
a lesson not lost on both of us; his
blasphemy had deemed me
more powerful than Neptune,
cleverer than King Canute –

Go on. Please
call me a dyke.

Faggot

He says, 'Faggots, man. Took me *a while* to be okay with them.
But lesbians... never had a problem with lesbians. Heh heh
　　heh.'

If you ever address me directly,
forget you think lesbians are sexy.
That you can somehow decide
dykes are fine while gay men vile –

Please. Say what you mean.
If you hate gay men, then you hate me.
So name me faggot.

Faggot. Noun, meaning bundle of twigs.

Faggot. Noun, meaning contemptuous term for a woman.

Faggot. Noun, meaning offensive and disparaging reference
to a male homosexual.

You claim your words are 'just figurative'. That there's
no linking hate to hate crime statistics. But each time you
say 'faggot' others use that as excuse to bash faggots
while standing up for your views.

You say 'faggot' like there's no consequence.
Like others aren't inspired by the ire you spit.
To us Stonewall isn't a convenient surface for
violence. You can't act like these attacks
aren't actively happening.

Faggot. Noun, fifteenth century, meaning bundle of twigs.
Specifically, the sticks used to set fire to heretics.

Faggot. Noun, sixteenth century, meaning contemptuous
term for a woman. Inferring from twig definitions this
references women as something awkward that
has to be carried. Meaning baggage. Meaning burden.
Meaning worthless.

Faggot. Noun, twentieth century, offensive and disparaging
reference to a male homosexual, which to some means
less than human, means carte blanche excuses to get
violent and abusive.

Keep the word 'faggot', but mind how you use it.
Meaning changes through evolving usage; what
started as wood would grow through using. Twigs
branched out to meanings abusive.
We don't need to redefine. Words don't stay rooted.
In time we'll have resown the seeds of its uses.

In origin, faggot twigs were lit and burned to ground,
then ashes turned the term to women. Burdens unbundled,
women whittled new beginnings. No longer worthless, the
term yet again shifted. Gay men came victim.
Love is fuel to flame when twigs turn matchstick wicked.

But through history, these ashes have led to same vision:
Each time, revived, a fiercer phoenix has risen.

I'm Sorry You're Wrong

An apology poem to my friend Ben, who believes women should wear
nothing but lingerie.

To the girl walking down Princes Street one
unseasonably warm May morning four years ago,
dressed in a loose white T-shirt and baggy jeans
with an old canvas record bag slung over
your left shoulder –
you had the merest suggestion of lace panties
unwittingly peeping over the top of your jeans.
That innocently misplaced display of lace
remains one of the sexiest things I've ever seen.

And to the girl who tormented me in high school
from inside the depths of that over-sized hoodie
you stole from an ex-boyfriend, arousing in me the
desire to see your mysteries which lay beneath:
three years later, post-freshman summer term,
you wearing your Uni Dance Team shirt
as I admired your fabric-hidden curves only
visible when you turned to reach your drink,
you said it'd look better on my bedroom floor –
it did.

But after years of having to imagine it
your bare skin was... heavenly.
See, I'm attracted to possibility,
intrigued by mystery, prefer girls
whose physiques I can't easily see;
the suggestion of cleavage, the hint
of lingerie. Not on display to openly titillate.

Ben says he loves it when the skin comes out,
considers summer his favourite season for
precisely this reason. But then, Ben has
an internet porn addiction and
hasn't had a girlfriend since 2006.
Personally, I like what I can't see. I enjoy imagining,
and when you've been previously kept to fantasy
there are few things as sexy as when her shirt
hits your bedroom floor.

Relative Memory

When she was younger, my grandmother could
disassemble and rebuild an army jeep.
Blindfolded. In less than twenty minutes.
These days, twenty minutes of lucidity recede
into her disassembling and rebuilding her life
without the right memories.

This Christmas, I sat next to her on the
dilapidated sofa that's been in our family
for generations, bubbling up old memories
for me like the pan of boiling water
when my grandpa used to cook
homegrown sweetcorn. But that
sofa means nothing to my gran.
Neither does my grandfather.

As we sat surveying the room of her family,
she pointed out each person and asked me
who they were.
Repeatedly.
For an hour.

Alone in a room, surrounded by relatives
loudly remembering, she sits unseeing
these fleeting histories of forgotten meaning:
daughters' engagements, great vacations,
family celebrations, her presence is...
vacant.

My grandmother's memories are like
a month-old birthday balloon lost
under the bed. Wrinkled, withered –
empty. All the air has been let out
of the tires of that army jeep
she deconstructed at seventeen, and she –
she no longer remembers her war.
The first of many she fought
in a long lifetime

That living room is empty, now.
Dust sheets have been draped over furniture,
shutters fastened tight across windows, and,
save twenty-minute bouts of lucidity, my grandmother
sits alone in a corner. Disassembling her memories.
Surrounded by family
                    unable to help her rebuild them.

Jump

David cried in class today.

Second period French spent watching
La Haine. The film ends with this sentiment:

A man fell from the seventeenth story of a tenement,
and with each floor he fell he said,

'Jusqu'ici, tout va bien.'

'So far, so good.'
Because it's not the landing that counts,
but the journey down.

Hiding in the forest at lunch time David
clutches the vodka bottle with trembling fingers,
speaking in whispers his shaking free-verse-
shaped pictures of deep hurt.

His cousin worked on the 101st floor,
World Trade Centre, Tower North.
The plane's impact three levels below
began an unyielding, imprisoning inferno.
The stairs down a no-go, Dave's cousin
had no way out but through windows.

Dave discloses he hopes he chose it, to
take control of the sole thing he had left –
the means of his end.

Chugging vodka remnants like it's
life-dependent, Dave says he can actually
see his cousin jumping from the window
actively pushing off
willingly throwing himself
into high-speed freefall.

Each millisecond closer to death
Dave hopes his cousin had said,
'So far, so good.'

David cried in class today.

Jusqu'ici, tout va bien.

Deserted Storm

Jay came back from Basrah with a video,
his very own snuff-film horror show; he
showed up back home with six months to
go on his third tour in a row. A PTSD-
shattered former human being, one-man
fighting machine reduced to scattered
tantrums and bad dreams. Initially
all we could see was the mate we'd always
known him to be, quietly sucking on a 40,
ignoring the hordes of imploring gazes and
invasive questions from his naïve mates.
Questions like:

So did you shoot anybody?

and

How many of them hajis did you kill?

'I want to show you something.'
Rising from his seat, Jay approached the TV.
Filmed from his perch in the tank's gun turret,
the DVD captured the first week's incursion.
Day one showed homes bombed down like
dominoes, cars explode, everything destroyed
in the tank's forward roll.

Day two showed dismembered torsos, pulps of skin and
shattered bone. Overturned cars were funeral homes,
rubble piles with lives inside became burning pyres.

By this point, the drinks had been put away.
Even the Backwoods blunts were stubbed out.
The room was totally silent
save the screams of agony and ammunition
thundering from the audio.
No one asked any more questions.
Somebody switched the film off.

But it was clear to all of us that
Jay was still watching.

Shades of Wrong, or 'How is the world still this fucked up?!'

My pale skin comes with unseen protection.
If race was sold by car salesmen, white
would be a factory standard pre-setting
for extra safety.

This 'gift' God gave me makes me
the Volvo of human beings,
but the cotton-swaddled auto-coddling
afforded by paler pigmenting
goes unnoticed by those who
never had to pick cotton
in the first place.

I am graced with the privilege
of this white face, firmly
placing me as perpetrator,
never victim, of racism.
Low-melanin skin gives me
easy living in every one
of this planet's cities.

It is a permanently worn
Kevlar vest, armour plating
never laid to rest, better protection
than being born in the West.
Want to give your kid the
best chance at life?

Make them white.

Dear Douche Canoe,

And by using the word 'douche' do not think for a
moment I even grace you with the compliment
of being shower-fresh
or by employing 'canoe' am bestowing on you
any false sense of buoyancy.
You, sir, are a douche canoe.

I say this because it is so much more
evocative than describing your recent
cowardice. For feck's sake, you have
a laptop, smartphone and a tablet;
how hard is it to send an email?!

Failing this, there are other ways
to send messages. Even a twelve-
year-old boy living in a cupboard
under the stairs somehow managed
to acquire an owl. Or are you so
unimaginative you can be outdone
by Harry sodding Potter?
Do the words 'carrier pigeon'
mean nothing to you?
How about smoke signals?
Semaphore? Sign language?
Jesus, man, even mime!

No, clearly the best thing to do
in any human interaction
is not to communicate, at all.

Total radio silence.

You utter douche canoe.

Values Meal

1. I wanted fried chicken. I wanted two women.
Neither of them were you.
While you were splashing in a rooftop pool
of gay men, I was in the gutter kissing your best friend.

Sometimes, pride means promiscuous.
Sometimes pride means acting out
scenes we can't be proud of.

I wanted fried chicken. I wanted two women.
I no longer wanted you.

2. On my last day yours will be the last face I want to see.
I don't mean that positively. Though it can be taken two
ways at once, once you realise there are two ways to take
this two-face, everything will be easier.

I wanted to not be chicken but
my brain was fried
from wanting two women,
and no one thought of you.

3. Two women walk into a fried chicken
joint and all either wants is the other.
The chicken is pretence. False intent.
An excuse. Half-nibbled bones thrown
to refuse, they excuse themselves
and head to a bedroom.

I wanted her.
She wanted the girl she was
in love with, but shuddering fingertips
traced the map of my wanting anyway.

4. There are two women. They stay satiated,
sweat dripping in the heat of no air conditioning.
As my girl's best mate lies naked in the aftertaste
of our misbehaving, I trace the truth of this
situation in the space now staking claim
'twixt our undressed shapes.

5. There are two women.
They stay guilt-ridden in separate cities.
The space formerly claiming their naked
shapes now encases moral misgivings.
The truth stays hidden. Full of their
shared cowardism, there is no room
for chicken.

Two-Faced Love

I fell in love so easily, so completely,
I couldn't see that for her, it was different.
Though she loved me with a passion
she never knew existed, we caused
contradictions of her long-held visions, like
white dresses. White picket fences.
A new last name after three little letters

My love for her left me defenceless,
her love for me plagued her with questions,
an unwanted acceptance; her heart was
served with a side of resentment.
Which meant that any true union of
us two was perpetually prevented.
She said,

'If you were a guy I'd have proposed to you by now.'

Without exception the worst sentence ever said to me.

But three years on… I get what she means.
One day, I want a family. And I've
never dreamed of store-bought semen,
medical treatments, assisted conceiving.
White paper sheets, white legal release,
a sterile setting wiped clean of any real
feeling with a resulting human being only
genetically linked to the one 'receiving treatment'.

That's not an appealing scene of conceiving.

Fast-forward a few years to the unthinkable:
an intensive care unit where I can't hear news
'til your family chooses to put me in the loop.

And maybe –
maybe that's too much for me.
Maybe I need love to be simpler than that.
When I dreamt ahead I only once pictured
a chick next to me, but she chose to live
life heterosexually, and if it can't be her
why not pick what's easy?

See… this is what scares me.
That I might make the same decision,
start discounting women before
a thing's even beginning, miss
out on real feeling 'cause I let myself
turn into the same coward she is.

But I might.
And my entire life
would become
so much
easier.

Lassies' Response

A Burns Night poem.

I don't know what I'd do without my boyfriend.
On him I do so deeply depend, for what use is
the kitchen if not to feed him? And I've never
used any other room in this house. He would
be the perfect spouse: a man's man, excelling in doing –
nowt.

All my dreaming's of cooking and cleaning.
These are what give a real woman meaning.
A life in his service 'til his wrecking my cervix
brings kids to increase my servantly purpose.

Oh how I yearn for it, these years ahead when
all the hair lost from his head is well represented
by those nose and back tufts instead. His former
six-pack's been upgraded to 'keg' –

Oh God I'll want him to take me to bed.

Speak to me of the Premier League,
whisper sweet cricket scores in my ear.
Oh, baby!

I will make you roast dinners like your mother used to,
I will separate your whites faithfully, just promise me
you will only ever scratch your testes in my presence.
You sexy, sexy man. I beg of you:
come home completely blotto and pee all over the
toilet seat. It means so much to me that this time
you actually used the bathroom.

And when you give me crisps and a
ten-pack of ciggies for our anniversary –
it means everything that you would drive
around at 4 am looking for an all-night gas station.
The day after our anniversary. That's so romantic!

You know what is romantic? He knew
my day had been shit. I walked in to find
each candle lit, he'd freshly cooked
my favourite dish –

When tasked to write on men from
the irreverent side I had no choice
but to generalise; I was forced to
rely on stereotype 'cause the
men in my life are dignified.

Asshole

I am an asshole.

This is not debatable,
more a statement of fact,
the backlash of recent events
preventing me from ignoring
such a shameful admission
given without desire for forgiveness.

As already said, this is a statement of facts.

Act one occurs in the usual terms
of drunken gropings and few words,
U-turns to nervous dates with
too much to say before returning
to bed and months of having sex all day.

Act two breaks with lesbian bed decay.
I no longer see you that way but because
I'm being kind it's too cruel to say.
Crueller than just *not* sleeping with you,
bulk-buying pyjamas and switching on
to the 6 am shift at work because I'm
being kind. And in the frankly fetid
recesses of my mind, this is the right
thing to do. Because you have too much
work due or any number of a thousand
excuses that preclude me from having to –
anything.

This relationship is in stasis,
a friendship ticking over like something
cryogenically frozen, a shared bed and
brief kisses used as our primordial soup,
hoping that bubbling under the surface

tension of our strained nothings a
working relationship is coming to life.
I fish for answers but nothing bites and
'nice' flies out the window.

If it wasn't already established that
I am an asshole, it's about to be inarguable.

Act three beckons with sexual tensions
between me and others too numbered
to mention. You can only last so long
in a sexless relationship before you start
to look elsewhere.
Which is when you end it.
Cue weeks of her speaking to my answering
machine while I drunkenly flirted with –

See, that's the problem. If it'd been half of
Glasgow it wouldn't have been so bad.
Repeatedly cheating with just one other
is being a very different kind of unfaithful
even if I didn't fuck him.

There is no point to hold in my favour,
no saving grace. This is not a debate,
more a statement of fact:
whilst I am an asshole,
I fear it's worse than that.

This is a statement
on how a coward acts.

On White People Saying Racism Is Dead In America

'I don't know what it is to be black,
to have slaves in my family three lifetimes back,
but the civil rights movement ended decades ago
and racism doesn't really exist any more.'

I have heard that excuse mouthed profuse
from too many pompous, naïve, rich white
youth when the truth is it's the same shit on
a different day. They locked up multiple black
kids in 2006 in Jena. Sent to the Louisiana
Pen facing ten to twenty-two for attempted murder two
on what was really a playground beatdown
after white kids hung nooses from a tree
'cause black kids hung loose one hot afternoon
beneath.

Someone told me racism was dying in America.

A young white man hiding an illegal loaded gun
in his trouser band held up three black kids for fun
at an empty gas stand; they rushed the man,
grabbed his piece then fled the street.
They were charged with theft, assault
and fleeing the scene while the white
boy with the concealed weapon walked away free.

I heard racism was dying in America.

Three New York police were acquitted of the
murder of Sean Bell who hours before his
wedding fell innocent victim to their firing
squad, killed in a hail of fifty gunshots,
popped for being clocked as a black man in a dark spot
so he must be rocking a Glock, *that cat is strapped*,
and yet the bureaucrat rap denies any racism involved
in this 'regrettable mishap'.

Sean Bell was killed, his friend Benefield
took three shots and months to heal while
Guzman will now only move on wheels.
Three innocent lives ruined for celebrating,
unarmed, one night. A firefight lighted
by prejudiced hype, profiling black guys
as gunmen, always carrying somethin'.

They tell me racism's dying in America.

It's been over a century since the abolition of slavery
but nooses are still being hung on trees,
cases like Sean Bell's keep hitting the streets
and white people keep refusing to see
that racism *is* dying in America.

Guilt

The night before the shit hit the fan,
Mike and I were lying on my roof, star-gazing,
lazily caning through a KB eighth.

'Yo, you going to that party in Virginia
tomorrow night? 'Cause this kid
Rodrigo'll give us a free ride,' he said.

The next evening I'm set for leaving
when the phone rings: Milly, calling
from Manchester to check in. Back
home, we had a thing brewing so
when Rodrigo's car pulled in, I told
him I'd make tracks with Max, but
thanks for the offer.

When Max and I finally got to the party,
Mike was nowhere to be seen, no one
knowing where he'd been, cell phone
straight to messaging.

Post-party day three, we found out on TV.
The newscaster set the scene:
Rodrigo drove, his seventeen-year-old girlfriend
and Mike in tow. Halfway to the party,
he parked the car. He vacated, no explaining,
so Mike and the girl stayed and waited.

Thirty minutes later, Rodrigo returned
without a word, burning rubber
as he sped out the suburb.

The two passengers knew nothing
'til the bright white of the police
searchlight confirmed the copter
overhead was for them.

Still, Rodrigo said nothing.

It wasn't 'til Interview Room 3
when confronted with crime scene
photography that Mike knew where
Rodrigo had been: nearly a mile
and a half away, killing a kid of fourteen
over a brick of weed.

But that was in Virginia, and they'd
driven from DC. Crossing state lines
rendered it a federal crime with
mandatory minimum sentencing
guidelines defining Mike as
'present at the scene of the crime'
and therefore tried as if he, too
had pulled the trigger.

Mike's crime was taking a free ride
from the wrong guy. As, but for a
phone call, so would've I.

Mike's sentence was life.

Moment of Silence

Suddenly the phrase 'Muscles from Brussels'
no longer had me thinking Van Damme but 'Goddamn'.
His grip around my neck too tight to fight,
the sudden apparition of a knife,
the first feel of cold steel, danger real, no help appeal –
dragged into a dark alley, a harsh reality,
a fourteen-year-old introduced to true brutality.
A rough cuff to the side of my head
slamming it back against red brick,
feeling sick, he pulls out his –
I won't continue with the imagery,
force you to live through the blue movie
that plays on constant loop through my memory.
I leave all that behind, try to find a future
in the time that I'm presented with.
Still I keep waking nights from dreams
of his fist, his kiss, his rhythm,
his violence, my silence, the pitiful shower-drip
that was never equipped to rid me of the
filthy products left by his mushroom tip.
It has been eight years of showers and I'm still not clean,
eight years of moving on and I'm still demeaned,
and he's still free but – that's down to me.
I couldn't face a court case: a quick-paced
defence lawyer bringing my family disgrace
with outright lies of my supposed sexually salubrious ways.
The thought of telling my father his daughter's
innocence got slaughtered on his watch,
my mother some guy prised my thighs
wide to the satisfied sighs of his cock.
I opted to keep my silence, somehow survive this,
no longer allow my loss of innocence
to rob me of my future of brightness, now
my future despite this, to right this, to slight this.

My reaction to your action is to overcome.
Your attempt to leave me with self-hatred
has only left me numb. I am stronger now,
not weakened by the thrusting of your phallic gun.

My reaction to your action is to overcome.

After Words

When I moved to Vietnam you took a Sharpie
and wrote 'mine' on my breasts. That was two
years ago but, baby, some nights I swear I can
still see those letters spelling you into my skin.
With new lovers blindly tracing the map you laid
on my body I think, *For your next girl, write it in braille.*

See, this is not a missive.
Me standing in a room you aren't in
begging, 'Take me back.'
I have no desire to go back.
This is for the loves that don't get to last,
that flash of glory in our failed pasts.
Baby, we were great together. Sometimes.
All those days you didn't want to kill me?
Those were awesome.

Remember Italy?
We'd curl up together on the David steps,
Florence lighting up the dusk below.
It would've been so romantic –
if the two-euro bottle of red wine
hadn't been picked by me.
It had even turned fizzy.

I wrote you a love poem once,
describing you as voluptuous.
Showed it to you when it got published.
You thought I'd called you chubby in public.

We spoke in different languages.
I thought I got it without understanding this,
not uncommunicative, just using dissimilar dialects.

We were the almost made-its.
So perfect, on some occasions.

Those arms carried me through
two years of broken sleep, nightmares
screaming me awake from traumatic dreams.
On the rare nights I wake nowadays I confess
I miss the safety I found in your embrace.
Baby, some nights those arms saved me.

This is not a missive.
This is me standing in a room you aren't in
saying, 'Thank you,'
and, 'Have an amazing life full of everything
you ever dreamed of 'cause you deserve it,'
hoping that one day, somewhere, you might hear this
and maybe, buried deep in the layers of your skin,
you carry a fading signature that says,
'I loved this girl, and it was beautiful.
And you should too.' But this piece of skin?
This small patch is taken.
It carries the memories we created
and it says 'Thank you'
traced in the letters of my name.

Lira

The war surrounds this place. Stages
night raids on boarding school gates,
forcing soldiers of the underaged
to swell the ranks of the LRA.
'Round here, fireworks are weapons-grade,
ordinance displays auger the end of day.
While the rest of us would tremble, quake –
these residents resist with dancing displays.

There is no artist who can capture the artistry
of these swiftly moving feet, the dancing in the street,
two-stepping to the other side of... fear.

There is music everywhere:
six men play a twenty-one-foot xylophone.
The generator powers a radio.
Life in these streets bubbles on overflow.
Their response to guns is to dance,
tango 'round bomb blasts,
twirl and sway past dud grenades
'til their rhythm of resistance
makes child's play of war games.
They will trace the cadence of liberation
in loose movement of body over music,
use djembes to drown out
the sound of war drums, 'til
every day becomes a party,
each beating of feet raising
two fingers to meet the
violence night brings.

Fear can be a choice you make,
resistance is a mental state
and this place will never capitulate
'cause when the new day breaks –
those left begin dancing.

Seeds

Did you know that seeds never die?
Even after decades dry, when
placed in water they will grow. In most
third-world countries the leading cause of
non-war-related death is water.

> So even seeds lose hope.

As typic as the image, gun barrels are never cold.
The first time I felt a muzzle jammed into my back
all I could think was, *How warm this is*.

Have you ever witnessed a bullet travelling
through the body? Know we crumple round the
bullet hole; we do not fall. We drop.

When you see someone's head cut off
their legs keep moving. When that head
hits the ground, it will roll 'til it lands
on neck stump, staring up –
sometimes, those new-dead eyes are all I see.

In Nakasemi I met three men who earned their living
driving continuously 'round the city shovelling corpses
off the street. They had been doing this so long they
tossed gun-shot battered bodies into back of pick-up
truck like sacks of muck. They told me after more than
twenty years of war, bodies are just carcass. I asked
if they thought post-death our souls left us; they said
souls are the last casualties of war, the thing you fight
hardest for, lost more quickly in the living than the dead.

House & Garden

By age five I'd lived in three countries,
been new kid on first school day four times,
twisted my young tongue round two languages,
tripping over tenses; everything was tense.
Like the tension felt in slack vines snapped
tight. Swinging from tree to tree, I
was our travelling circus's monkey.
New house to new flat in new country,
the only constant my family tree we less-
than-carefully uprooted. Young saplings
never had time to bloom new shoots before
we shovelled up foundations, replanting
somewhere new. We never saw spring flowers
burst through same ground twice; I –
have never had a home, not known
where I'm supposed to come from,
could only guess where we were headed.
'Next' defined my adolescence.
The only things we never threw away
were cardboard boxes and packing tape.
My life had to fit into one quarter of a moving crate.
There are no knick-knacks in my history,
no keepsakes, no treasures from my
childhood days. As I watched everything
I cared about get tossed away, they'd say,
'All you need are your memories.'

I remember the first time I felt safe.

I was 28.

I am 28.

Her arms wrapped round my waist,
my face pressed into her neck.

That exhaled breath held decades
of everything I'd repressed. The heft
of never having anything to count on,
no constancy to cling to: I never knew
how hard it was to bear that weight
'til that first day I didn't have to.

I want to plant seeds with you,
give spring saplings space
to mature from shoots.
I want the luxury of roots.

I've never had a home, so
don't know how to build one
but, darling, maybe one day
you and I can grow a garden.

Acknowledgements

This is not an autobiography; it's a collection of stories. Some are mine, some were borrowed, all are true. To everyone I've ever raised a glass with, ranted at, or tripped over, thank you. But without Tina Thuermer, Kevin Cadwallender, Ross Sutherland, Brittany Fonte, Jenny Lindsay, Bram Gieben, Kath McMahon, Marlous Smits, Nicole Brandon, DonMike Mendoza, Young Dawkins, Michelle Madsen, Matt Panesh, Rachel Rosen, Regie Cabico (and if you haven't read Regie's poem 'Check One', you're missing everything), DeAnn Emett, Fay Roberts, Lucy Ayrton, Smithy and a few others (you know who you are, you wonderful humans), I'd have never written in the first place. And to Mum and Dad, because who knew parents could be that supportive and enthusiastic about this disastrous a career choice?

9 781909 136427